MYSQL Programming Professional Made Easy

By Sam Key

Expert MYSQL Programming Language Success in a Day for any Computer User!

2nd Edition

Table of Contents

Introduction

I want to thank you and congratulate you for purchasing the book, "MYSQL Programming Professional Made Easy: Expert MYSQL Programming Language Success in a Day for any Computer User!"

This book contains proven steps and strategies on how to manage MySQL databases.

The book will teach you the fundamentals of SQL and how to apply it on MySQL. It will cover the basic operations such as creating and deleting tables and databases. Also, it will tell you how to insert, update, and delete records in MySQL. You will also learn how to test your code. In the last part of the book, you will learn how to connect to your MySQL server and send queries to your database using PHP.

Thankfully, by this time, this subject is probably a piece of cake for you since you might already have experienced coding in JavaScript and PHP, which are prerequisites to learning MySQL.

However, it does not mean that you will have a difficult time learning MySQL if you do not have any idea on those two scripting languages. In this book, you will learn about SQL, which works a bit different from programming languages.

Being knowledgeable alone with SQL can give you a solid idea on how MySQL and other RDBMS work. Anyway, thanks again for purchasing this book, I hope you enjoy it!

Chapter 1: Introduction to MySQL

This book will assume that you are already knowledgeable about PHP. It will focus on database application on the web. The examples here will use PHP as the main language to use to access a MySQL database. This will focus on Windows operating system users.

As of now, MySQL is the most popular database system by PHP programmers. Also, it is the most popular database system on the web. A few of the websites that use MySQL to store their data are Facebook, Wikipedia, and Twitter.

Commonly, MySQL databases are ran on web servers. Because of that, you need to use a server side scripting language to use it.

A few of the good points of MySQL against other database systems are it is scalable (it is good to use in small- or large-scale applications), fast, easy to use, and reliable. If you are already familiar with SQL, you will not have any problems in manipulating MySQL databases.

Preparation

In the first part of this book, you will learn SQL or Standard Query Language. If you have a database program, such as Microsoft Access, installed in your computer, you can use it to practice and apply the statements you will learn.

In case you do not, you have two options. Your first option is to get a hosting account package that includes MySQL and PHP. If you do not want to spend tens of dollars for a paid web hosting account, you can opt for a free one. However, be informed that most of them will impose limitations or add annoyances, such as ads, in your account. Also, some of them have restrictions that will result to your account being banned once you break one of them.

Your second option is to get XAMMP, a web server solution that includes Apache, MySQL, and PHP. It will turn your computer into a local web server. With it, you can play around with your MySQL database and the PHP codes you want to experiment on. This comes with phpMyAdmin. A specific tool will be discussed later in this book.

Advantages of MySQL

MySQL is more popular among web developers compared to most programming languages. It is widely used because its size and speed is ideal for all kinds of websites. Also, it is open source. For those who are not familiar about internet jargon, “open source” means the program or database can be used for free and a global community of programmers are trying to contribute to improve its features. Here is a list of the advantages of using MySQL:

1. **It is user-friendly**. Unlike other databases, which require complicated coding and programming, MySQL database allows users to build and interact with the program even by just knowing a few key SQL statements. The SQL language is best known for it being the standard language used for RBDMSs that will be discussed in detail in Chapter 3.
2. **It is inexpensive**. Not only is this database inexpensive, it is free as part of the GPL license. For commercial or business use however, the price is reasonable.
3. **It is fast**. For internet uses, especially when developing a website, developers require a fast-acting database that can store loads of data. In fact, the designer of MySQL

has speed as his main goal while developing the software.

4. **It can adapt to many operating system**. MySQL is designed to match to run in many operating systems. It is universally coded to make sure that it can run on (a) Windows, (b) Mac OS, (c) Linux, (d) Unix or other less popular operating systems.
5. **It can be used in different Web hosts.** Unlike other databases that are compatible only with certaub Web hosts, MySQL can be used in almost any Web hosting service available in the network.
6. **It is secure.** It has a special feature that allows selective but flexible authorization privileges for specific users or groups. Passwords can be encrypted in the system.
7. **It has an organized Technical support.** Regardless of wherever you are in the world, MySQL has a large group of users offering free support in mailing lists. Often, MySQL developers participate in support discussions.
8. **It is customizable.** Unlike other databases, MySQL is completely customizable mainly because of the GPL license that allows different programmers to personalize the software for desired use.

How MySQL Works

Several utility programs including the MySQL server comes with the MySQL software. Other supporting software that aid in the maintenance and administration of MySQL databases is also used when performing specific tasks in the system.

The MySQL server is the core of the whole MySQL system. It manages all the function of the system by handling all the input instructions in designated databases. For example, when creating new sets of databases, you will have to code a message that instructs the MySQL server to create a new database and call it 'NewInfo.'

The MySQL server will create a new subdirectory called `NewInfo` and inputs all the new data inputs into the `NewInfo` subdirectory. When sending input data to server, you can ask the MySQL server to file the new input data in a specific subdirectory.

Before sending instructions to the MySQL server, it must be online and running. Instructions won't be sent and executed when the server is down. The MySQL server is set up in such a way that it runs while the main frame starts and continues running to allow data input anytime. This complements how Web sites are set up.

The server does not necessarily have to be set up so that it starts when the computer is turned on. It can be programmed to start only when needed to access the MySQL databases. While the MySQL server is running, it will listen for any coded messages you send it.

Chapter 2: The MySQL Server

As explained in the previous chapter, all interactions made with the MySQL database are facilitated by sending coded messages into the MySQL server. There are several ways to send message to the MySQL server but the most prominent way is by using PHP, which will be widely discussed in the last chapter. The PHP software utilizes simplified statements that can be used to send specific coded instructions to the server.

In order to carry out the instructions you send, the MySQL must be able to comprehend the language you used in coding your messages. This is where the SQL (Structured Query Language) comes in. This language is understood by many RBDM (relational database management systems), which will be discussed in detail in the next chapter.

Simply, the MYSQL server can break down SQL into understandable parts to comprehend the message. PHP cannot do this but PHP's role is to lay down the wires to connect the MySQL server by sending the specific SQL message via this connection.

Once received, the MySQL server retrieves the SQL message and executes the instruction. The MySQL will notify you about the status of the execution by sending a message prompt through the same PHP pipeline. It will also send an error message once it wasn't able to understand or execute the instructions.

The MySQL server manages your database by: (a) creating new databases, (b) organizing data and where they are stored, and (c) storing and retrieving information based on requests or queries coded in the instructions you send.

The following sections will describe how to build an SQL query and transmit it through the MySQL servers.

Building SQL Queries

SQL is almost English as the language is specifically engineered mainly by using English keywords put together to form different words that can appear similar to how you often phrase your sentences. There is no need for you to learn a different technical language in order to understand how SQL queries work.

In each query, the first word is the query's name. The name serves as the command word (usually a verb) which instructs MySQL how to execute the input data. In the succeeding chapters, you will learn more about command words including: `CREATE`, `DELETE`, `UPDATE`, `DROP`, `LOAD`, `INSERT`, `SELECT`, and `ALTER`. Knowing how each keyword functions will suffice in creating and interacting with databases for different websites.

Input words or phrases follow the command words. These input words will serve as the data for the MySQL server. For example if you want MySQL to `CREATE`, you must tell it which database or entry you want to `CREATE`.

Here is an example of a query:

```
SELECT firstName FROM MemberList
```

This query will derive the first names of the names listed in the table called `MemberList`. There are complicated queries that might not resemble readable English sentences. For example:

```
SELECT firstName, FROM MemberList WHERE
    country="USA" AND city="New York"
    ORDER BY firstName
```

This particular query will derive all the first names of the people who live in New York City, United States of America whose names are listed in the `MemberList` table. The query might not follow English syntax but the instruction is still clear.

Here are some points that you should keep in mind when creating an SQL query:

1. **Capitalization.** This will be discussed extensively in Chapter 5 but most reserved words in the SQL languages does not require being capitalized but for the purpose of this book, most of the reserved words are in uppercase letters to differentiate them from input data that will be in lowercase letters. When using SQL, `FROM` is the same as `from` however when using Unix or Linux, columns or table names are different when using different cases. For example, `MemberList` is different from `memberlist`. When using Windows, both names can be used interchangeably.
2. **Spacing.** SQL words require at least one or more space of separation. It does not however differentiate whether you are using more than one space. It does not make a distinction whether you write the whole statement in just a single line or use separate lines to encode new information.
3. **Quotes.** In the example above, the words, `USA` and `New York` are both enclosed by quotation marks (""). MySQL requires quotation marks to denote text strings or character strings.

Sending SQL Queries

There are two ways to send SQL queries to the server when building a web-based application. These are:

1. phpMyAdmin. This software is especially developed to manage MySQL databases. This software runs in a browser and is coded using PHP. This software makes MySQL more user-friendly by providing a simple interface that improves how you interact with the MySQL server.

2. PHP scripts. Specifically invented to send SQL queries, PHP language is developed to contain features that allow users to send and receive information.

These two ways will be discussed in the last chapter.

Chapter 3: The MySQL Database

A MySQL database is an application or a file wherein you can store data. It is used and it comes with almost all types of computer programs. A database is usually present in the background whether the program is a game, a word processor, or a website.

A database can be a storage location for a player's progress and setting on a game. It can be a storage location for dictionaries and preferences in word processors. Also, it can be a storage location for user accounts and page content in websites.

There are different types and forms of databases. A spreadsheet can be considered a database. Even a list of items in a text file can be considered one, too. However, unlike the database that most people know or familiar with, those kinds of databases are ideal for small applications.

A database includes two parts: the data itself and the structure that houses the data. Most applications require users to create a new set of table for the influx of new information. For business applications for example, applications tend to require users to create new table to store information about a new customer.

Creating a New Database

Using phpMyAdmin interface, you can create an empty database. After the creation of a new database, you can now start adding new tables that contain information to the newly created database. Here is how to create a new database:

On your local computer

1. In your browser, open the phpMyAdmin homepage.

2. Click on the Create New Database heading located on the lower left column of the main menu.

3. In the blank space provided, key in the desired name of the new database.

4. Click Create.

On your Web Host

1. Locate the control panel, which is often located at the home page of your Web Host.

2. Click the icon representing MySQL databases. A new page will open to allow you to create a new database. This page will list all your live databases.

3. In the space provided, type the name of the new database you want to create.

4. Click on the "Create Database" prompt.

Viewing a Database

When you need to check on a particular database and the information stored to it, you can just go to the main page of phpMyAdmin. The page lists down the names of the live databases that can be opened anytime. Beside each name includes a number that denotes the number of tables contained in each database.

When using SQL, you can use this query:

```
SHOW DATABASES
```

Deleting a Database

Using phpMyAdmin, you can delete a particular database by:

1. Go to the main page of phpMyAdmin.

2. On the list of live database, click the database you want deleted.

3. The page will then display the name of the database. This will show you the list of tables stored inside the database. Click Drop.

4. Click Okay.

A prompt will tell you that the command has been performed. It will also show you the executed query:

```
DROP DATABASE deleteddatabase
```

In the above query, the database named '`deleteddatabase`' is already deleted by the MySQL server.

It is important to remember that when using the command `DROP`, the executed instruction is irreversible. In other words, when a database is deleted, it can no longer be retrieved as it is gone for good. It also follows that all data stored in it is gone forever.

For Web hosting accounts, Web hosting companies have different policies in the deletion of databases. For open source database, the database may have been deleted from your account but it may still exist in the company's server for their future use.

BONUS: Adding Tables to Database

Whether it is an existing database or a new database, you can add tables to organize information within each database. In many cases, phpMyAdmin is a heavy favorite because of its user-friendly interface.

For example, a database called `ShirtCatalog` can be designed with three distinct tables including: `Shirt`,

`ShirtBrand`, `ShirtSize`, `ShirtColor`, and `ShirtCut`. In order to follow through with the example, consider these steps:

1. Name your database. In this example, the name of the Shirt Catalog is `ShirtCatalog`.
2. Identify the information that your database will require to be supplied by users. For example:
   - Brand name of the shirt
   - Different sizes available
   - Shirt colors available
   - Types of cuts available
   - Price
3. For each object, you need to name the table.
4. Identify the specific details for each attributes of each object.
   - *Brand Name*. This identifies the brand name of the shirt in the inventory.
   - *Shirt Identification Number*. This is a sequence number systematically assigned to each shirt entered in the system.
   - *Shirt Size*. This identifies the sizes available for each shirt.
   - *Shirt Color*. This identifies the particular shade available for each shirt.
   - *Type of cut*. This identifies the type of cut available for each shirt.

- *Price*. This is the dollar equivalent of each shirt in the inventory.

5. Define and name the column entries.

   The `Shirt` table should produce one row containing information for each pet. The columns of the `Shirt` table should include:

`shirtID`	This stores unique numerical sequence assigned for each stock.
`shirtBrand`	This stores brand names of each shirt in stock.
`shirtSize`	This stores the size of each shirt. ("`XS`," "`S`," "`M`," "`L`," "`XL`")
`shirtColor`	This stores the color of each shirt.
`shirtCut`	This stores specific tailor cut of each shirt.
`shirtPrice`	This stores the price of each shirt.

6. Identify the primary key for the `Shirt` table.

   In the example, the primary key of the `Shirt` table is `shirtID`.

7. Define defaults if any.

8. Identify which particular columns should require input data:

   In the example, you could pick which items should not left blank when storing required information. For example:

   - `shirtID`
   - `shirtBrand`

- `shirtCut`

If the user leaves any of these values blank, the database would not generate entry for the shirt item.

RDBMS

The type of database that is commonly used for bigger applications is RDBMS or relational database management system. MySQL is an RDBMS. Other RDBMS that you might have heard about are Oracle database, Microsoft Access, and SQL Server.

Inside an RDBMS, there are tables that are composed of rows, columns, and indexes. Those tables are like spreadsheets. Each cell in a table holds a piece of data. Below is an example table:

id	username	password	Email	firstname	lastname
1	Johnnyxxx	123abc	jjxxx@gmail.com	Johnny	Stew
2	Cutiepatutie	qwertyuiop	cuteme@yahoo.com	Sara	Britch
3	Mastermiller	theGear12	mgshades@gmail.com	Master	Miller
4	j_sasaki	H9fmaNCa	j_sasaki@gmail.com	Johnny	Sasaki

Note: this same table will be used as the main reference of most of the examples in this book. Also, while developers usually encrypt their passwords in their databases, this example does not use any encryption method.

In the table, which the book will refer to as the "`account table`" under the sample database, there are six columns (or fields). They are labeled as "`id`," "`username`," "`password`," "`email`," "`firstname`," and "`lastname`." As of now, there are only four rows. Rows can be also called entries or records. Take note that the first row is not part of the count. They are just there to represent the name of the columns as headers.

An RDBMS table can contain one or more tables.

Compared to other types of databases, RDBMS are easier to use and manage because it comes with a standardized set of method when it comes to accessing and manipulating data. This method is SQL or Standard Query Language.

Chapter 4: Standard Query Language (SQL)

Before you start learning MySQL, you must familiarize yourself with SQL or Standard Query Language first. SQL is a language used to manipulate and access relational database management systems. It is not that complicated compared to learning programming languages.

Some of the things you can do with databases using SQL are:

- Get, add, update, and delete data from databases
- Create, modify, and delete databases
- Modify access permissions in databases

Most database programs use SQL as the standard method of accessing databases, but expect that some of them have a bit of variations. Some statements have different names or keywords while some have different methods to do things. Nevertheless, most of the usual operations are the same for most of them.

A few of the RDBMS that you can access using SQL – with little alterations – are MySQL, SQL Server, and Microsoft Access.

At the advent of powerful programming platforms and environments like Visual Studio.NET and Visual Basic programmers find that learning the basics of coding SQL statements and queries is a good skill to possess. The availability of powerful and carefully-coded database engines including the MySQL Server Express Edition encouraged many users to brush up their skills in using SQL.

Most of these users include professional developers who already have their resumes filled with experiences in using various types of programming language. Some individuals who already considered experts in their fields will suddenly find themselves coding database applications for business applications.

Considered as one of the leading SQL software, the MySQL Server Express offers a free use of various database applications and more advanced databases than its pears. It enjoys the same database core mechanism as its predecessors only that this time, the software has a better build that allows smoother setup and easier distribution without having to empty your pockets.

SQL supports all recently-released advance database features including triggers, stored procedures, views, full SQL support, and native XML support. Several tools can help you design queries visually. A good example is the Visual Database Tools platform, which is made available through Microsoft Visual Studio.

Despite the existence of these tools, knowing and understanding how to read and write SQL language is still important. The benefit in understanding how the visual tools perform their job is crucial in utilizing their full capacity. Often, manually coding the SQL statement is the simpler (sometimes even the faster) way to tell the server to perform a specific set of instructions. This also opens the doors into learning the full capabilities of relational databases.

Relational Databases

In the previous chapter, you were already given a glimpse of how Relational Databases work through RDBMS. Aside from the example provided in the previous chapter, it is important to know that there are many types of relational databases but you only need to know about the general type.

A relational database is comprised of different tables. Each table is comprised of different rows or records of data. The data stored in each row is classified according to defined discrete variables of information known as columns or fields. Here is an example:

EmployeeID	Surname	First Name	Middle Name
201412721	Saunders	Philip	Lockwood

Each database can have different links or relationships which can have a one-to-many or one-to-one correspondence. This correspondence will serve at the link between data information stored in each table. The connection or links between tables in the same database is engineered by defining the relationship between a Primary Key and a Foreign Key. The Foreign Key in any given table will correspond to the Primary Key of another table to form a correspondence.

For example, the relationship between the variables, `CUSTOMERS` and `ORDERS` enjoy a one-to-many relationship. The `CUSTOMERS` and `ORDERS` table both have a `CUSTOMERID` variable, which will serve as the Primary Key for the `CUSTOMERS` table and as the Foreign Key for the `ORDERS` table. The `CUSTOMERID` links the two tables in the same database accounting for every transaction made. This way, the server will not require having to provide the exact same name of customers, it will use the number sequence stored in `CUSTOMERID` to link the two tables together.

Chapter 5: SQL Syntax

SQL is like a programming language. It has its own set of keywords and syntax rules. Using SQL is like talking to the database. With SQL, you can pass on commands to the database in order for it to present and manipulate the data it contains for you. And you can do that by passing queries and statements to it.

SQL is commonly used interactively in databases. As soon as you send a query or statement, the database will process it immediately. You can perform some programming in SQL, too. However, it is much easier to leave the programming part to other programming languages. In the case of MySQL, it is typical that most of the programming is done with PHP, which is the most preferred language to use with it.

SQL's syntax is simple. Below is an example:

```
SELECT username FROM account
```

In the example, the query is commanding the database to get all the data under the username column from the account table. The database will reply with a recordset or a collection of records.

In MySQL, databases will also return the number of rows it fetched and the duration that it took to fetch the result.

Case Sensitivity

As you can see, the SQL query is straightforward and easy to understand. Also, take note that unlike PHP, MySQL is not case sensitive. Even if you change the keyword SELECT's case to select, it will still work. For example:

```
seLeCT username from account
```

However, as a standard practice, it is best that you type keywords on uppercase and values in lowercase.

Line Termination

In case that you will perform or send consecutive queries or a multiline query, you need to place a semicolon at the end of each statement to separate them. By the way, MySQL does not consider a line to be a statement when it sees a new line character – meaning, you can place other parts of your queries on multiple lines. For example:

```
SELECT
username
FROM
account;
```

New lines are treated like a typical whitespace (spaces and tabs) character and the only accepted line terminator is a semicolon. In some cases, semicolons are not needed to terminate a line.

Chapter 6: SQL Keywords and Statements

When you memorize the SQL keywords, you can say that you are already know SQL or MySQL. Truth be told, you will be mostly using only a few SQL keywords for typical database management. Also, almost half of the queries you will be making will be SELECT queries since retrieving data is always the most used operation in databases.

Before you learn that, you must know how to create a database first.

CREATE DATABASE

Creating a database is simple. Follow the syntax below:

```
CREATE DATABASE <name of database>;
```

To create the sample database where the account table is located, this is all you need to type:

```
CREATE DATABASE sample;
```

Easy, right? However, an empty database is a useless database. You cannot enter any data to it yet since you do not have tables yet.

CREATE TABLE

Creating a table requires a bit of planning. Before you create a table, you must already know the columns you want to include in it. Also, you need to know the size, type, and other attributes of the pieces of data that you will insert on your columns. Once you do, follow the syntax below:

```
CREATE TABLE <name of table>
(
```

```
    <name of column 1> <data type(size)>
<attributes>,
    <name of column 2> <data type(size)>
<attributes>,
    <name of column 3> <data type(size)>
<attributes>
    );
```

By the way, you cannot just create a table out of nowhere. To make sure that the table you will create will be inside a database, you must be connected to one. Connection to databases will be discussed in the later part of this book. As of now, imagine that you are now connected to the sample database that was just created in the previous section.

To create the sample account table, you need to do this:

```
CREATE TABLE account
(
id    int(6)    PRIMARY    KEY    UNSIGNED
    AUTO_INCREMENT PRIMARY KEY,
username varchar(16),
password varchar(16),
email varchar(32),
firstname var(16),
lastname var(16),
);
```

The example above commands the database to create a table named account. Inside the parentheses, the columns that will be created inside the account table are specified. They are separated with a comma. The first column that was created was the id column.

According to the example, the database needs to create the id column (id). It specified that the type of data that it will contain would be integers with six characters `(int(6))`. It specified some optional attributes. It said that the id column will be the primary key of the table and its values will `AUTO_INCREMENT` – these will be discussed later. Also, it specified that the integers or data under it will be "unsigned", which means that only positive integers will be accepted.

MySQL Data Types

As mentioned before, databases or RDBMS accept multiple types of data. To make databases clean, it is required that you state the data type that you will input in your table's columns. Aside from that, an RDBMS also needs to know the size of the data that you will enter since it will need to allocate the space it needs to store the data you will put in it. Providing precise information about the size of your data will make your database run optimally.

Character Data

This is the most common type of data stored in the MySQL database. This data puts together different strings of characters together. If used for business, most of the pieces of information are character data. For example, customer name, nickname, address, customer type etc. This type of data can be printed as an output or added together (concatenated).

There are two formats where this kind of data can be stored:

1. **Fixed-length**: MySQL prepares a fixed number of spaces specific for this data. If the data string is shorter than the preset number of spaces, extra spaces will be left empty and thus, wasted. If the data string is longer than the preset number of spaces, only the characters that fit will be stored.

For example, for a column defined as PASSWORD, you defined that the number of spaces is 10 characters. Consider the following:

Input Data	Number of Char.	Stored Data
ABC123	6	ABC123
ABCDE12345	10	ABCDE12345
ABCDEF123456	12	ABCDEF1234

2. Variable-length: Regardless of length or number of characters, MySQL stores the same number of characters as input value.

Numerical Data

Just like character data, this is another common type of data. This includes decimal numbers (0.0005, 3.1416, 8999.01) and integers (5, 78, 1009, 123434). Data stored as a number can be used in performing mathematical equations including addition, subtraction, multiplication, division, squaring etc. Otherwise, the data will be stored as a character string. A good example of numbers that should be stored as character strings are phone numbers, zip codes because you will never have to perform mathematical equations using those kinds of data.

Data and Time Data

This is another common data type. There are several date formats that can represent specific or arbitrary date and time.

Enumeration Data

There are data that can only include a specific or limited number of data. For example, if the value requires a choice between `yes` or `no`. This allows you to tell MySQL specific values that can be stored in the particular column. For example, if there are only red and blue shirts available, then you can tell MySQL that the choice is only between `red` and `blue`. No other values will be stored in the database.

Data Type Names

Below are some of the data types that you can store in a MySQL database:

`INT(size)`	This is an integer data type. These are numbers without fractional components or decimal places. A column with an INT data type can accept any number between -2147483648 to 2147483648. In case you specified that it would be "unsigned," the column will accept any number from 0 to 4294967295. You can specify the number of digits with INT. The maximum is 11 digits including include the negative sign (-).
`FLOAT(size, decimal)`	This is float data type. These are numbers with fractional components or decimal places. These cannot be "unsigned." You can specify the number of digits it can handle and the number of decimal places it will store. If you did not specify the size and number of decimals, MySQL will set it to 10 digits and 2 decimal places (the decimal places are included in the count of the digits). Float can have the

	maximum of 24 digits.
`TIME`	The time will be stored and formatted as HH:MM:SS.
`DATE`	The Date will be stored and formatted as YYYY-MM-DD. It will not accept any date before year 1,000. Also, it will not accept date that exceeds 31 days and 12 months.
`DATETIME`	This is a combination of DATE and TIME formatted as YYYY-MM-DD HH:MM:SS.
`TIMESTAMP`	This is formatted differently from DATETIME. Its format is YYYYMMDDHHMMSS. It can only store date and time between 19700101000000 and 20371231235959 (not accurate).
`TIMESTAMP` `CHAR(size)`	This stores strings with fixed size. It can have a size of 1 to 255 characters. It uses static memory allocation, which makes it perform faster than VARCHAR. It performs faster because the database will just multiply its way to reach the location of the data you want instead of searching every byte to find the data that you need. To make the data fixed length, it is padded with spaces after the last character.
`VARCHAR(size)`	This stores strings with variable length size. It can have a size of 1 to 255 characters. It uses dynamic memory

	allocation, which is slower than static. However, when using VARCHAR, it is mandatory to specify the data's size.
`BLOB`	This store BLOBs (Binary Large Objects). Data is stored as byte strings instead of character strings (in contrast to TEXT). This makes it possible to store images, documents, or other files in the database.
`TEXT`	This stores text with a length of 65535 characters or less.
`ENUM(x, y, z)`	This allows you to specify the values that can be only stored.

INT, BLOB, and TEXT data types can be set smaller or bigger. For example, you can use TINYINT instead of INT to store smaller data. TINYINT can only hold values ranging from -128 to 127 compared to INT that holds values ranging from -2147483648 to 2147483647.

The size of the data type ranges from TINY, SMALL, MEDIUM, NORMAL, and BIG.

- `TINYINT, SMALLINT, MEDIUMINT, INT, and BIGINT`
- `TINYBLOB, SMALLBLOB, MEDIUMBLOB, BLOB, and BIGBLOB`
- `TINYTEXT, SMALLTEXT, MEDIUMTEXT, TEXT, and BIGTEXT`

You already know how to create databases and tables. Now, you need to learn how to insert values inside those tables.

INSERT INTO and VALUES

There are two ways to insert values in your database. Below is the syntax for the first method:

```
INSERT INTO <name of table>
VALUES (<value 1>, <value 2>, <value 3>);
```

The same result will be yield by:

```
INSERT INTO <name of table>
(<column 1>, <column 2>, <column 3>)
VALUES (<value 1>, <value 2>, <value 3>);
```

Take note that the first method will assign values according to the arrangement of your columns in the tables. In case you do not want to enter a data to one of the columns in your table, you will be forced to enter an empty value.

On the other hand, if you want full control of the INSERT operation, it will be much better to indicate the name of the corresponding columns that will be given data. Take note that the database will assign the values you will write with respect of the arrangement of the columns in your query.

For example, if you want to insert data in the example account table, you need to do this:

```
INSERT INTO account
(username, password, email, firstname,
    lastname)
VALUES
("Johnnyxxx", "123abc", "jjxxx@gmail.com,
    "Johnny", "Stew");
```

The statement will INSERT one entry to the database. You might have noticed that the example did not include a value for the ID field. You do not need to do that since the ID field has the AUTO_INCREMENT attribute. The database will be the one to generate a value to it.

SELECT and FROM

To check if the entry you sent was saved to the database, you can use SELECT. As mentioned before, the SELECT statement will retrieve all the data that you want from the database. Its syntax is:

```
SELECT <column 1> FROM <name of table>;
```

If you use this in the example account table and you want to get all the usernames in it, you can do it by:

```
SELECT username FROM account;
```

In case that you want to multiple records from two or more fields, you can do that by specifying another column. For example:

```
SELECT username, email FROM account;
```

WHERE

Unfortunately, using SELECT alone will provide you with tons of data. And you do not want that all the time. To filter out the results you want or to specify the data you want to receive, you can use the WHERE clause. For example:

```
SELECT <column 1> FROM <name of table>
WHERE <column> <operator> <value>;
```

If ever you need to get the username of all the people who have Johnny as their first name in the account table, you do that by:

```
SELECT username FROM account
WHERE firstname = "Johnny";
```

In the query above, the database will search all the records in the username column that has the value Johnny on the firstname column. The query will return Johnnyxxx and j_sasaki.

LIMIT

If you only need a specific number of records to be returned, you can use the LIMIT clause for that. For example:

```
SELECT <column 1> FROM <name of table>
LIMIT <number>;
```

If you only want one record from the email column to be returned when you use SELECT on the account table, you can do it by:

```
SELECT email FROM account
LIMIT 1;
```

You can the LIMIT clause together with the WHERE clause for you to have a more defined search. For example:

```
SELECT username FROM account
WHERE firstname = "Johnny"
LIMIT 1;
```

Instead of returning two usernames that have Johnny in the firstname field, it will only return one.

UPDATE and SET

What if you made a mistake and you want to append an entry on your table? Well, you can use UPDATE for that. For example:

```
UPDATE <name of table>
```

```
SET <column 1>=<value 1>, <column 1>=<value 1>,
<column 1>=<value 1>
WHERE <column> <operator> <value>;
```

In the example account table, if you want to change the name of all the people named Master to a different one, you can do that by:

```
UPDATE account
SET firstname="David"
WHERE firstname="Master";
```

Take note, you can perform an UPDATE without the WHERE clause. However, doing so will make the database think that you want to UPDATE all the records in the table. Remember that it is a bit complex to ROLLBACK changes in MySQL, so be careful.

DELETE

If you do not to remove an entire row, you can use DELETE. However, if you just want to delete or remove one piece of data in a column, it is better to use UPDATE and place a blank value instead. To perform a DELETE, follow this syntax:

```
DELETE FROM <name of table>
WHERE <column> <operator> <value>;
```

If you want to delete the first row in the account table, do this:

```
DELETE FROM account
WHERE id = 1;
```

Just like with the UPDATE statement, make sure that you use the WHERE clause when using DELETE. If not, all the rows in your table will disappear.

TRUNCATE TABLE

If you just want to remove all the data inside your table and keep all the settings that you have made to it you need to use TRUNCATE TABLE. This is the syntax for it:

```
TRUNCATE TABLE <name of table>;
```

If you want to do that to the account table, do this by entering:

```
TRUNCATE TABLE account;
```

DROP TABLE and DROP DATABASE

Finally, if you want to remove a table or database, you can use DROP. Below are examples on how to DROP the account table and sample database.

```
DROP TABLE account;
DROP DATABASE sample;
```

Chapter 7: Protecting Your Data

Perhaps more than the structure that houses data, the data itself comprises the most important chunk of any Web database application. Valuable time has been spent developing the database to include all the information it possesses. Some of which contains important details entered by the users of the database. This information can be vulnerable to outside threats including those who want to mine data from your database especially when it contains confidential information such as passwords, credit card and social security numbers.

Controlling Access

When your database includes sensitive information, the need for controlling who has access to this information should be a priority. You also have to decide who can change the data stored in the database to preserve the integrity of the application. Most of your competitors will want to pry on your data or even change the information included in your online catalog to their advantage. The moment you let your guard down, your competitors can not only just destroy your database but they can also procure a copy of your customer list. Once this happens, your business will lose its competitive advantage and you will be brought to your knees in no time.

Fortunately, MySQL devised an encrypted security system that prevents users from hacking through the system and mine sensitive information thereby protecting your data. MySQL can require users to create an account to access data in the database however having an account does not guarantee access. Only the system administrator can determine which accounts can have access to the information.

Each MySQL account should contain the following:

- A name
- A password
- A *hostname*. This is the machine imprint on the account to gain access to the MySQL server.
- A specific set of privileges.

In order to access the data in the database, a user must have a validated account that has registered credentials:

- Username
- Password

As an added security measure, the person must access the database only from a computer whose IP is granted access to the database. The computer credentials must complement the specific account credentials; otherwise, the access will be voided.

Once a user is allowed access to the database, the amount of activity of the user is limited by the privileges set by the system administrator for the account. Each account is provided with only a unique set of privileges including any of the following: `DROP`, `CREATE`, `INSERT`, `DELETE` or `SELECT`. The settings or permission can be modified by the administrator anytime using a master account that has access to all MySQL processes.

If you are the system administrator, you can set up accounts that have full privileges, no privileges or a mixture of both. For example, customer accounts can only access information printed in the online catalog but they won't be able to edit out the information.

There are two stages where MySQL controls access to sensitive data when executing an SQL query. These are:

1. **Connection verification**. MySQL issues a checking mechanism to determine the validity of the account credentials. This also checks whether a particular user is accessing the database from a secured connection and a computer that was already given clearance. Once all the details are verified, MySQL will accept the connection.

2. **Request verification**. After giving clearance to a connection, MySQL will check on the list of privileges set to the account. If the account attempts to perform a set of instructions that are beyond the list of privileges, MySQL will not execute the query. An error notification will notify the user that he lacks the necessary privilege to access the query. If the query falls within the list of privileges, MySQL will execute the query.

Account Names and Hostnames

When identifying a unique account, MySQL verifies the account name and hostname. Hostname is the designated name of the terminal that is given clearance to have an established connection with the database. It is important to remember that there can be many different accounts containing the same name but with a different hostname. However, there can be different accounts bearing the same name containing the same hostname.

Here are some other things that you should bear in mind about MySQL account names:

1. **Account names can be as long as 16 characters.** It can include special characters such as a hyphen or even a space. Wildcards can't, however, be used in account names.
2. **Account names can be blank**. If a blank account name exists in the MySQL server then any account can be valid for that particular account. If a user is accessing through the same hostname that is cleared for the blank account (and that he knows the correct password), the user can use any account name. This can also be tweaked to allow users to access your database.
3. **Hostnames can be an IP address or a name**. For example, hostnames can be `captainamerica.marvel.com` or it can also be an IP address like `192.163.0.22`. The `localhost` is the machine where the MySQL server is installed. Unlike account names, host name can include a wildcard.

Passwords

It is important that every account have its own password. If you don't want to require passwords then you can leave the password as blank. MySQL does not require any particular length for passwords although there are certain applications that may limit the passwords to only ten characters. All succeeding characters will be dropped.

As an additional security, MySQL encrypts credentials before it stores them to a more secured database. In other words, user credentials are stored in varying characters that won't be easily recognized unless decrypted with a specific key. This security feature makes sure that no one can mine passwords from the secured database where all MySQL credentials are stored.

Unfortunately, hackers have invented several means to guess your password. They created software that allows a practice called cracking. It rapidly enters different passwords successively until it arrives with the correct combination.

Here are key tips to avoid being hacked:

1. Never use a date or a phone number.
2. Never include names of your loved ones, especially not yours.
3. Never use a word that can easily be tied to you. This can be place or residence, street where you live, name of a pet, name of a favorite character.
4. Never include a word that can be found in English or foreign dictionary.
5. Never use a variation of your account name.
6. Utilize all the letters allowed by the application.
7. Vary your password using a combination of lower case letters, uppercase letters, punctuation marks and numbers.

The best passwords are those that are hard to guess but easy to remember. If the password is hard to remember, you should put it in a piece of paper although this defeats the purpose of using passwords.

Account Privileges

The good thing about MySQL's security system is that it can grant users only specific account privileges in order to preserve the integrity of the database. Not everyone who can access the database is allowed to do everything, or anything at all except access it. For instance, a user account can be set up to insert data but not delete or drop data.

These privileges are clearance levels that can be granted for tables, columns or databases. For example, a user account can be set up to allow the user to select data from the whole database but only insert or update information only in specific columns in specific tables within the database.

Systems administrator can grant the following privileges to particular user account at any given time:

Privilege	**Clearance level**
`ALL`	User is granted full privileges. This is usually the clearance level for system administrators.
`ALTER`	User is allowed to alter table structures.
`CREATE`	User is allowed to create new tables or databases.
`DELETE`	User is allowed to delete or remove rows from tables.
`DROP`	User is allowed to drop tables and databases.
`FILE`	User can create and verify information from the MySQL server.
`GRANT`	User can give clearance or alter clearance level of various MySQL accounts.
`INSERT`	User is allowed to insert rows containing new information into the tables.
`SELECT`	User can verify and read data from databases.
`SHUTDOWN`	User is allowed to close the MySQL server.

`UPDATE`	User can change and update data in the database.
`USAGE`	User enjoys no access to the MySQL server.

Remember that granting ALL to certain users may prove to be a bad idea because this includes privileges that are exclusive for administrative management including shutting down the whole MySQL server.

Setting Up MySQL Accounts

When setting up and MySQL accounts, there is only one account required, that is the account tied to your computer. Web hosting companies have varying naming conventions although most follow this format:

```
domain@localhost
```

For now, you don't need to think a lot about hostname. The Web host will show you that information on your phpMyAdmin landing page. Usually IT providers will provide you with the account name and hostname.

The most important thing for you to remember is that you only need to create another account with limited privileges to allow you access from different computer terminals.

Adding Accounts

The best way to connect to MySQL using PHP is by setting up an account that grants this purpose. Another way to create an account is to send an SQL queries using INSERT or UPDATE command to the MySQL database housing credential information. This database is created upon the installation of MySQL. Most Web hosts do not provide access to the database so the best way to add an account is by accessing the phpMyAdmin interface. If the web hosts fail to interact with the MySQL credentials database, it will notify you via an error messages that says:

```
Access denied for user 'xx'@'localhost'
    to database 'mysql'
```

Instead of providing direct access to the MySQL database, Web hosts provides a specific page in their platform created just for the creation and management of various accounts. The control panel icons allow you to control and set privileges to these accounts.

Here are the steps on how to add accounts using the control panel used by several Web hosts:

1. Open the control panel by clicking the home page of your Web host account.
2. Locate the icon representing the MySQL databases. Click it.
3. Click the icon that says, "Jump to MySQL Users." This is usually located in the upper right corner of the control panel. Another way of accomplishing this step is by scrolling down to the section that says, "MySQL Users."
4. In the Username field, key-in the new account name.
5. In the Password field, key-in desired password. One of the new features of this page includes a metric that measures the strength of the password. It follows an algorithm that measures how effective the password can protect the account.
6. In order to verify that you remember the password you typed, type the password in the "Password (Again)" portion.
7. Click on the "Create User" button.

8. Click "Return" to proceed to the MySQL home page.

Allowing Access to Database

This important procedure must be kept in mind in protecting all your data. This section allows you to choose which accounts will be given particular access.

1. Proceed to the MySQL User portion of the database page.
2. Select a user from the dropdown list.
3. Select a particular database that you want the user to have access.
4. Click the "Add" button.
5. Among the list of privileges, check the boxes corresponding to the privilege you want the account to have clearance.
6. Tap on the "Make Changes" button.
7. Return to the MySQL database homepage.

Changing Privileges

There are a few times when you feel that you have to limit the privileges a particular account enjoys prompting you to make changes in the level of clearance the account has.

1. Open the control panel in your account.
2. Locate the MySQL database icon. Click it.
3. Scroll down until you reach the "Current Databases" portion of the page.
4. Find the specific row that you want to alter privileges for.

5. Select the account name you wish to modify or change privileges for.
6. Select the box adjacent to the each listed privilege you want to add or remove.
7. Tap on the "Make Changes" button.

Adding or Changing Passwords

Passwords are optional but they are necessary when you want to keep your database secured. Adding or changing passwords can be made in an existing account.

When changing passwords, you can begin by adding the account again. Follow the steps provided in the previous sections of this chapter. In the section that allows you to create a new account, just type in the account name and then type the password in both fields that require it then click "Add User."

When you want to use SQL to change password directly through the MySQL server, you can send something similar to this:

```
SET PASSWORD FOR accountname@hostname =
    PASSWORD{"newpassword"}
```

Since most Web Hosts don't allow direct access to the MySQL database server, you can expect an error message that says:

```
Access denied for user 'xx'@'localhost'
    to database 'mysql'
```

Removing Accounts

Follow any of the steps above to access the list of usernames. In one of the adjacent columns, you will find a red x that deletes the account. In order to remove the account, click on the x adjacent to the account name.

Data Back Up

There are times when the MySQL system is compromised. This may lead to loss of data and other pertinent information that your system requires in order to work. These problems may arise not necessarily due to coding or system error; sometimes, external threats hacking through your database can pose a threat to your system.

It is for this reason that developers like you should keep at least a backup copy of your database. There is no foolproof system to protect your data and some of your harshest competitors might play dirty even to the point of committing company espionage.

Also, disasters like the computer where the database is kept can be vulnerable especially while processing a big chunk of data. Once the computer breaks down, there is a big possibility that you will lose all your data. Incidents like the computer file being stored in the system might contain a worm that can infest and eat your system out or fortuitous situations like the building where the computer is stored can burn down. While these events are less likely to happen, it is better to err on the safe side. Keeping a backup copy of your database protects you from averting the complications from the disasters.

The good thing about Web hosting companies is that most of them back-up the database stored in their system on a periodic basis. If your website is stored in the company server, the IT personnel is responsible for keeping a copy of the site. Most companies follow a back up procedure performed regularly. In order for you to know how your company does the procedure, you can always talk with the IT department and inquire how regularly they perform backup procedures. It is important that you are aware of the backup procedures so you are aware how much of the data is secured in a separate system in case something happens to the live system.

Aside from being contented with the backup procedures performed by your Web hosting company, another security measure that you may want to take is keeping another backup to your local computer or network. This way, you are sure that you have a triplicate copy of your database. Also, if done on a more regular basis, you are confident that close to 100% of your data is stored in a local storage device. When disaster strikes, the process of replacing the damaged database is faster since you can easily access your local network compared to having to rely on your Web hosting company to sort out the issues on their end.

If your Web site is designed to collect information from users, you can code your site to simultaneous back-up new information on your local network or computer. This way, your Web site sends data information not only to the Web hosting company but also to the backup storage within the confines of your own home or office. Hence, when you are in the process of establishing and testing your site, the actual database used is stored within the local network making the information tenfold safer.

In other words, it is recommended that you have a triplicate copy of your database. One of which is the live database. The other two copies are either stored through the backup procedures of the Web hosting site or into your local computer.

Most web hosting companies store their backup in a different server to prevent any complications from affecting all their data. Some of them may also store a backup copy in an offsite computer, which can take time to access. With a backup copy in your computer, this will save you time, effort and money from having to deal with a third-party company to retrieve and recover lost files.

Exporting your data (phpMyAdmin)

When exporting data, you can use your phpMyAsmin platform to make a backup copy of your database stored by your Web hosting company:

1. Open the homepage of phpMyAdmin.

2. Among the list in the left portion of the phpMyAdmin page, select the database that you want to backup.

3. Click the tab named "Export" located at the top portion of the page.
4. Once the "Export" page opens, go to the left pane of the main control panel. Among the listed tables in the panel, choose the tables you want to backup by clicking on the empty boxes beside them.

5. Select the "SQL radio" key at the bottom of the Export page.

6. Choose the "Structure" empty box and the other empty boxes located at the upper portion of the Structure section. Make sure there's a check inside the box that indicates the selected options.

7. If not already selected, put a check on "Select the Data" empty box.

8. If not already selected, put a check on "Use Hexadecimal for Binary Data" empty box.

9. Locate the "File" section, which is usually at the bottom of the screen.

10. Put a check on the "Save as File" empty box.

11. Key in the desired filename inside the space provided. Make sure that this file name is easy to recognize when you must access the file on a later date. The template of the File Name contains "`__DB__`" which means this file will serve as the database name. phpMyAdmin allows to add special characters or text to the current filename to differentiate the two filenames. As a tip, you may want to add the date and time of backup so it will be easier for you to recognize the latest backup file.

12. Put a check on the "Remember Template" empty box.

13. In the "Compression" portion of the page, click on the "None" button.

14. Click on the "Go" button. Once your browser's "Save File" prompter opens, you will be notified of the filename of the copy being saved.

15. Choose the option that allows you to save the file to your local disk then click "OK." The file will then be stored at wherever your browser is set to save downloaded files. To double-check, you can navigate through the file manager and check if your backup file is successfully saved there.

Chapter 8: Testing MySQL

In order to test if MySQL is running without any glitch, you can test MySQL accessibility by using the PHP platform. This test should check whether your development environment and your Website are receiving and storing the information into your database. The usual first step is to run a test using your developmental site in the local network and the usual second step is to upload the same file to your site before you run another test there. Here are the steps to perform this procedure:

1. Create this file, "`mysql_testfile.php`" anywhere within your Web space environment. You can choose any filename for as long as it will be easy for you to differentiate the test file from the rest of the files.
2. Run the file in the main directory or subdirectory depending on which directory you want to run the test.
3. Code this into your file:

```
<?php
/* Program Type: mysql_testfile.php
    * Description:
    * This program tests the MySQL
Server
    * connection and
    * outputs settings.
    */
Echo(1) "<html>
<header>
<title>Test File MySQL</title>
</header>
```

```
        <body>";
        $hostname = "localhost";
        $username = "mysqluseraccount";
        $pass = "mysqluserpassword";
        $cnx =
mysqli_connect($hostname,$username,$pass);
        $code = "SHOW DATABASES";
        $product = mysqli_query($cnx,$code;
        if($product == false)
        {
        Echo(1)
        "<h3>Error Report:
".mysqli_error($cnx."</h3>";
        }
        else
        {
        if(mysqli_num_rows($product) < 1)
        {
        echo "<p>No stored database
available</p>";
        }
        else
        {
        echo "<li>";
        while($code =
mysqli_fetch_row($product))
        {
        echo "<ol>$code[0]</ol>";
        }
        echo "</li>";
        }
        }
        ?>
        </body>
        </html>
```

4. Execute mysql_testfile.php. If an error message appears then there is something wrong with the MySQL server. Fortunately, the error prompt notifies you about the problem the server is experiencing so you can troubleshoot accordingly.

Chapter 9: MySQL and PHP

You already know how to manage a MySQL server to the most basic level. Now, it is time to use all those statements and use PHP to communicate with the MySQL server.

To interact or access a MySQL database, you need to send SQL queries to it. There are multiple ways you can do that. But if you want to do it in the web or your website, you will need to use a server side scripting language. And the best one to use is PHP.

In PHP, you can communicate to a MySQL server by using PDO (PHP Data Objects), MySQL extension, or MySQLi extension. Compared to MySQLi extension, PDO is a better choice when communicating with a MySQL database. However, in this book, only MySQLi extension will be discussed since it is less complex and easier to use.

Connecting to a MySQL database:

Before you can do or say anything to a MySQL server or a database, you will need to connect to it first. To do that, follow this example:

```
<?php
    $dbservername = "localhost";
    $dbusername = "YourDataBaseUserName";
    $dbpassword = "YourPassword12345";

    // Create a new connection object
    $dbconnection            =            new
    mysqli($dbservername, $ dbusername, $
    dbpassword);
```

```
// Check if connection was successful
if ($dbconnection->connect_error) {
    die("Connection failed/error: " .
$dbconnection->connect_error);
}
echo "Connected successfully to
database";
?>
```

In this example, you are using PHP's MySQLi to connect to your database. If you are going to test the code in the server that you installed in your computer, use localhost for your database's server name.

By the way, to prevent hackers on any random internet surfers to edit or access your databases, your MySQL server will require you to set a username and password. Every time you connect to it, you will need to include it to the parameters of the mysqli object.

In the example, you have created an object under the mysqli class. All the information that the server will send to you will be accessible in this object.

The third block of code is used to check if your connection request encountered any trouble. As you can see, the if statement is checking whether the connect_error property of the object $dbconnection contains a value. If it does, the code will be terminated and return an error message.

On the other hand, if the connect_error is null, the code will proceed and echo a message that will tell the user that the connection was successful.

Closing a connection

To close a mysqli object's connection, just invoke its close() method. For example:

```
$dbconnection->close();
```

Generating a different MySQL Database

```
<?php
    $dbservername = "localhost";
    $dbusername = "YourDataBaseUserName";
    $dbpassword = "YourPassword12345";

    // Create a new connection object
    $dbconnection             =            new
    mysqli($dbservername, $ dbusername, $
    dbpassword);

    // Check if connection was successful
    if ($dbconnection->connect_error) {
        die("Connection failed/error: " .
    $dbconnection->connect_error);
    }

// Creating a Database
$dbSQL       =       "CREATE       DATABASE
    YourDatabaseName";
if   ($dbconnection->query($dbSQL)    ===
    TRUE) {
    echo "YourDatabaseName was created.";
}
else {
    echo "An error was encountered while
    creating    your    database:    "    .
    $dbconnection->error;
}
$dbconnection->close();
    ?>
```

Before you request a database to be created, you must connect to your MySQL server first. Once you establish a connection, you will need to tell your server to create a database by sending an SQL query.

The $dbSQL variable was created to hold the query string that you will send. You do not need to do this, but creating a variable for your queries is good practice since it will make your code more readable. If you did not create a variable holder for your SQL, you can still create a database by:

```
$dbconnection->query("CREATE DATABASE
YourDatabaseName")
```

The ***if statement*** was used to both execute the query method of `$dbconnection` and to check if your server will be able to do it. If it does, it will return a value of TRUE. The ***if statement*** will inform you that you were able to create your database.

On the other hand, if it returns "false" or an error instead, the example code will return a message together with the error.

Once the database was created, the connection was closed.

Interacting with a Database

Once you create a database, you can now send SQL queries and do some operations in it. Before you do that, you need to connect to the server and then specify the name of the database, which you want to interact with, in the parameters of the mysqli class when creating a mysqli object. For example:

```
<?php
    $dbservername = "localhost";
    $dbusername = "YourDataBaseUserName";
    $dbpassword = "YourPassword12345";
```

```
$dbname = "sample"

    // Create a new connection object
    $dbconnection              =            new
    mysqli($dbservername, $ dbusername, $
    dbpassword, $sample);

    // Check if connection was successful
    if ($dbconnection->connect_error) {
        die("Connection failed/error: " .
    $dbconnection->connect_error);
    }
    echo    "Connected    successfully    to
    database";
    ?>
```

phpMyAdmin

In case you do not want to rely on code to create and manage your databases, you can use the phpMyAdmin tool. Instead of relying on sending SQL queries, you will be given a user interface that is easier to use and reduces the chances of error since you do not need to type SQL and create typos. Think of it as Microsoft Access with a different interface.

The tool will also allow you to enter SQL if you want to and it will provide you with the SQL queries that it has used to perform the requests you make. Due to that, this tool will help you get more familiar with SQL. The best thing about it is that it is free.

On the other hand, you can use phpMyAdmin to check the changes you made to the database while you are studying

MySQL. If you do that, you will be able to debug faster since you do not need to redisplay or create a code for checking the contents of your database using PHP.

Using the phpMyAdmin interface is just a piece of cake. Here is an example on how to add a new table to your database:

1. Go to the main phpMyAdmin landing page.
2. Among the list of database in the page, choose one by clicking the name where you want to add a specific table to.
3. On the field provided, type the name of the new table.
4. Provide the number of fields or data figures you want your data table to contain.
5. Click Go.
6. Key in the definitions for each data figures.
7. Click Save.

Conclusion

Thank you again for purchasing this book!

I hope this book was able to help you to master the fundamentals of MySQL programming.

The next step is to learn more about:

- Advanced SQL Statements and Clauses
- Attributes
- The MySQLi Class
- PHP Data Object
- Security Measures in MySQL
- Importing and Exporting MySQL Databases
- Different Applications of MySQL

Those topics will advance your MySQL programming skills. Well, even with the things you have learned here, you will already be capable of doing great things. With the knowledge you have, you can already create an online chat application, social network site, and online games!

That is no exaggeration. If you do not believe that, well, check out the sample codes that experts share on the web. You will be surprised how simple their codes are.

Finally, if you enjoyed this book, please take the time to share your thoughts and post a review on Amazon. We do our best to reach out to readers and provide the best value we can. Your positive review will help us achieve that. It'd be greatly appreciated!

Thank you and good luck!

Check Out My Other Books

Below you'll find some of my other popular books that are popular on Amazon and Kindle as well. Simply click on the links below to check them out. Alternatively, you can visit my author page on Amazon to see other work done by me.

Android Programming in a Day

Python Programming in a Day

C Programming Success in a Day

C Programming Professional Made Easy

JavaScript Programming Made Easy

PHP Programming Professional Made Easy

C ++ Programming Success in a Day

Windows 8 Tips for Beginners

HTML Professional Programming Made Easy

If the links do not work, for whatever reason, you can simply search for these titles on the Amazon website to find them.

Made in the USA
Middletown, DE
08 February 2016